THE BRIGHT ROSE

To Eleanor

Every good wish

Philip

03 x 16

the Bright Rose
Early German Verse 800–1280

Edited and translated by
Philip Wilson

Arc
PUBLICATIONS
2015

Published by Arc Publications,
Nanholme Mill, Shaw Wood Road
Todmorden OL14 6DA, UK
www.arcpublications.co.uk

Translation copyright © Philip Wilson 2015
Introduction copyright © Philip Wilson 2015
Copyright in the present edition © Arc Publications 2015

978 1908376 71 8 (pbk)
978 1908376 72 5 (hbk)
978 1908376 73 2 (ebook)

Design by Tony Ward
Cover design by Tony Ward & Ben Styles
Printed in Great Britain by
TJ International, Padstow, Cornwall

ACKNOWLEDGEMENTS

Versions of some of the translations have appeared in
Ambit and *Modern Poetry in Translation*.

The translator owes a deep debt of gratitude to John
Gledhill, for introducing him to the world of Old and
Middle High German; to Ruth Harvey, for tutoring him
in its literature and for her comparison of *Minnesang*
with the sweet lyric of Cole Porter (*German Life and Let-
ters*, Volume 17 Issue 1); and to Chris Wells, for taking
him through Old High German linguistics. He would
also like to thank Jean Boase-Beier, Antoinette Fawcett
and Valerie Henitiuk for their encouragement, and all at
Arc Publications.

**'Arc Classics:
New Translations of Great Poets of the Past'
Series Editor: Jean Boase-Beier**

This anthology is dedicated to
Gareth Jones

TRANSLATOR'S NOTE

The decision to create this book came from reading anthologies edited by Leonard Forster, Ingrid Kasten, Stephan Müller and Hans-Joachim Simm. The texts follow those in the works below.

This is not a critical edition, and I have adopted editorial conjectures without indicating these in the German and without indicating textual variants. I have kept endnotes to a minimum because this is intended as a literary work rather than a work of scholarship. The order of the poems is chronological, although I have grouped the Old High German spells and verses together.

I have used the following sources:

Forster, L. (ed.) *The Penguin Book of German Verse* (London: Penguin, 1994);

Heinrich von Morungen, *Lieder* (Stuttgart: Reclam, 1975);

Kasten, I. (ed.) *Frauenlieder des Mittelalters* (Stuttgart: Reclam, 1990);

Müller, S. (ed.) *Althochdeutsche Literatur* (Stuttgart: Reclam, 2007);

Simm, H.-J. (ed.) *Liebesgedichte des Mittelalters* (Berlin: Insel, 2010).

CONTENTS

The present volume offers a selection of the earliest German poetry, from its beginnings until its medieval flourishing. The translations are from Old and Middle High German, terms that demand explanation. By 'High German', linguists designate the West Germanic dialects that underwent the Second Sound Shift, a change in pronunciation originating in the highlands of the south (hence 'High German') and which differentiated these dialects from Low German. The shift is still discernible if we compare contemporary English (the descendant of Low German) and contemporary German (the descendant of High German): thus English has 'pound', 'tame', 'daughter' and 'brother', where German has *Pfund*, *zahm*, *Tochter* and *Bruder*. The term 'Old High German' designates the shifted German language from the eighth century to the middle of the eleventh century, by which time the texts we possess have changed sufficiently to be labelled 'Middle High German'. By the time of Martin Luther (1483-1546), who translated the Bible, the language can be classified as New High German.

Old High German Verse

I heard it said that two men, champions, met between two armies and prepared to do battle, father and son... Or rather, I read it, in the *Hildebrandslied* [Song of Hildebrand], the oldest recorded poem in High German, represented by a single manuscript that has been dated at around 800, though it looks back to an older Indo-European past. The manuscript is incomplete and the result of the fight is not mentioned and must be inferred from similar stories in other languages, which indicates how precarious the survival of the oldest German literature is. We have the Roman historian Tacitus's assurance in the *Germania* that song was important to the Germanic tribes, but little has survived in written form; the poems we have and value

11

are typically the product of anonymous monks working in scriptoria, taking a break from the copying of sacred work in order to record poetry in their own dialects.

Even though few works of literary value are extant in Old High German, with nothing on the scale of the Anglo-Saxon *Beowulf*, what does remain can offer an album of a time and a way of seeing the world, through texts that continue to have poetic effects, both in the source language and – I hope – in translation. This anthology includes: the *Hildebrandslied*; the *Ludwigslied* [Song of Ludwig], a song of praise to a victorious king; the *Muspilli* (the word is of uncertain meaning), which describes the end of the world, a Christian vision that uses pre-Christian imagery; the 'Wessobrunner Gebet' [Wessobrunn Prayer], a remarkable attempt to describe the time before creation; a number of invocations, most of which are Christian but one pre-Christian; a few marginal annotations written on wet afternoons.

The poems offer an overview of a society in transition from a pagan worldview to a Christian one. The human form of life that is depicted is one we can still recognise. We can shiver as Hildebrand laments that a wicked fate is working itself out that will force him to kill the son who does not recognise him. We can marvel at the imagery of the world's end in *Muspilli*, whether or not we share the poem's Christian belief. And, in our world where bees are vanishing, we can sympathise with the beekeeper's spell for a swarm's return. Human nature may not have changed as much as the German language.

MIDDLE HIGH GERMAN VERSE

In contrast to Old High German Literature, a large corpus of Middle High German lyric poetry survives. It is possible, for example, to publish a whole volume of lyrics by Heinrich von Morungen, by whom more than thirty texts survive. The Middle High German period from the twelfth to the fourteenth century has been termed the *Blütezeit* [time of flourishing] by scholars. This was the world of the secular court, where the minstrel functioned as entertainer and instructor for his listeners. Longer poems have also survived, such as courtly romances by Gottfried von Strassburg, Hartmann von Aue, and Wolfram von Eschenbach, or the anonymous epic *Nibelungenlied* [Song of the Nibelung]. It would have been interesting to include excerpts from these works of poetic genius, but considerations of space mean that only complete shorter works have been chosen.

Middle High German lyric verse is represented here by eleven poets of the *Minnesang* [love song], of whom eight can be identified by name. The lyrics typically depict expressions of love to a lady, in the hope of reward. As the term *Minnesang* suggests, these texts would have been sung, but in most cases the music has been lost. We should not read the words too literally as a record of minstrels having their way with noble women, because *Minnesang* was a public performance rather than an expression of private passion. The *Nibelungenlied*, for example, contains an episode in which the minstrel Volker sings at court to a queen and is rewarded for his praises by a gift of bracelets, rather than by anything more intimate. The poets engage in a highly professional ritual, composing on the basis of cognitive metaphors that still ring true: LOVE IS A TRAP; LOVE IS A GAME; LOVE IS WAR. We continue to use these metaphors, as can be shown by juxtaposing *Minnesang* with a contemporary cultural phenomenon, the Eurovision Song Contest. Heinrich von Morungen (who died around 1220) wrote a song, included here, in which he tells his lady that she is a sweet assassin whose lack of care will surely kill her faithful servant, but that he will nonetheless continue to serve her, even beyond the grave. In Oslo, 2010, the German singer Lena Meyer-Landrut won the Eurovision with her performance of 'Satellite', in which she offers love the assurance that she will carry on loving, whether love is sweet or cruel. All the elements of *Minnesang* are here: public performance; cognitive metaphor; the power of love. The lyricists of the Middle Ages did, however, have other themes. I include, for example, a poem by Walther von der Vogelweide that laments growing old, and that exhorts his listeners to support the call to crusade of Frederick II.

THE TRANSLATION

In presenting this edition, I have been able – thanks to the philosophy of Arc Publications – to place my translations opposite the source texts, so that the translation can be shown at least to aim to represent the Old or Middle High German. The relative shapes of source and target text become relevant, whilst the reader with some knowledge of German will spot ancestors of contemporary vocabulary on the left-hand pages. The song form of *Minnesang* becomes apparent in the tightly constructed stanzas and often intricate rhyme schemes of the courtly lyrics. When translating, I have looked at each individual source text and formed a strategy accordingly. An example of this is the rendering of the Middle High German 'Owê' [alas]. In translating the first song here by Heinrich von Morungen, in which two lovers part at dawn, I have translated it as 'oh no', because it strikes me as what somebody might say in the circumstances. My translation of Walther von der Vogelweide's final poem here, however, uses 'alas', in order to preserve the game that Walther is playing with the single word. The lexical item 'Owê' is thus given two different renderings. Similarly, I have translated the Old High German 'welaga nu' in the *Hildebrandslied* as 'alas', in order to suggest the antiquity of that poem.

Most poems in this anthology use full rhyme, a consequence of their original setting as song lyrics. I have tried to suggest rhyme by a variety of techniques, from full rhyme to assonance, in order to show the highly formal nature of the corpus, although it should be remembered that the texts we possess are variants. In the world of performed poetry, every creation is a recreation, just as these translations are my creation of the world of the earliest German verse. Some of the Old High German texts show alliteration as a binding technique, and again this is suggested in the translations. Given that many of the poems in this anthology were originally composed as lyrics for oral performance, I have paid attention to the rhythms of the source texts and have attempted to produce target texts that also work rhymically. The caesuras of the poems are also important and have been retained.

A translated poem can attempt to play the same language-games as the poem it represents, to use a term from the philosopher Ludwig Wittgenstein's *Philosophical Investigations*. Two poems can stand in a relation of similarity to each other, as source and target text. The lyrics in this collection look back to ancient traditions and look forward to the modern German language and the modern world.

An anonymous Old High German manuscript annotation – given as the last of the four verses that end the first section – informs us that the annotated text was often read by Hicila the fair. Hicila, whoever she was, died long ago, but translation enables Old and Middle High German verse to continue to reach new audiences.

Philip Wilson

OLD HIGH GERMAN VERSE

DAS HILDEBRANDSLIED

Ik gihorta ðat seggen,
ðat sih urhettun   aenon muotin,
Hiltibrant enti Haðubrant   untar heriun tuem.
sunufatarungo   iro saro rihtun.
garutun se iro guðhamun,   gurtun sih iro suert ana,
helidos, ubar hringa,   do sie to dero hiltiu ritun,
I Iiltibrant gimahalta: hcr uuas heroro man,
ferahes frotoro;   her fragen gistuont
fohem uuortum,   hwer sin fater wari
fireo in folche,   …
…   'eddo hwelihhes cnuosles du sis.
ibu du mi ęnan sages,   ik mi de odre uuet,
chind, in chunincriche: chud ist mir al irmindeot.'
Hadubrant gimahalta,   Hiltibrantes sunu:
'dat sagetun mi   usere liuti,
alte anti frote,   dea erhina warun,
dat Hiltibrant haetti min fater: ih heittu Hadubrant.
forn her ostar giweit,   floh her Otachres nid,
hina miti Theotrihhe   enti sinero degano filu.
her furlaet in lante   luttila sitten
prut in bure,   barn unwahsan,
arbeo laosa: her raet ostar hina.
des sid Detrihhe   darba gistuontun
fateres mines: dat uuas so friuntlaos man.
her was Otachre   ummet tirri,
degano dechisto   miti Deotrichhe.
her was eo folches at ente: imo was eo fehta ti leop:
chud was her…   chonnem mannum.
ni waniu ih iu lib habbe'…

18

THE SONG OF HILDEBRAND

Two champions, father and son, must fight to the death

I heard it said,
that champions   singly met,
Hildebrand and Hadubrand,   between two armies,
a son and a father   preparing their armour.
They put on their war-gear,   they girded their swords on,
heroes, over ring-armour,   then they rode to battle.
Hildebrand spoke: he was the older man,
wise in life;   he began to ask
in few words   who his father was
in the clansfolk,   …
…   'or of what clan you might be.
If you tell me one,   I will know the others:
child, in the Kingdom   I know all the heroes.'
Hadubrand spoke,   Hildebrand's son:
'That was said to me   by our people,
old and wise,   who came before,
that Hildebrand was my father's name: I am called Hadubrand.
He went to the East,   he fled Odoaker's spite,
away with Dietrich   and many of his fighters.
He left in the land,   in distress,
a bride in the bower,   and an ungrown bairn,
robbed of inheritance: he rode off to the East.
Since then Dietrich   needed him badly,
my Father: he was so friendless a man.
He was to Odoaker   an endless enemy,
the truest fighter   with Dietrich.
He was always at the head of the folk:
    to him fighting was always dear.
Known was he…   to bold men.
Nor do I think that he lives'…

19

'wettu irmingot   obana ab hevane,
dat du neo dana halt mit sus sippan man
dinc ni gileitos'…
want her do ar arme   wuntane bauga,
cheisuringu gitan,   so imo se der chuning gap,
Huneo truhtin: 'dat ih dir it nu bi huldi gibu.'
Hadubrant gimahalta,   Hiltibrantes sunu:
'mit geru scal man   geba infahan,
ort widar orte.   …
du bist dir alter Hun,   ummet spaher,
spenis mih mit dinem wortun,   wili mih dinu speru werpan.
pist also gialtet man,   so du ewin inwit fortos.
dat sagetun mi   sęolidante
westar ubar wentilsęo,   dat inan wic furnam:
tot ist Hiltibrant,   Heribrantes suno.'
Hiltibrant gimahalta,   Heribrantes suno:
'wela gisihu ih in dinem hrustim,
dat du habes heme   herron goten,
dat du noh bi desemo riche   reccheo ni wurti.' –
'welaga nu, waltant got,   wewurt skihit.
ih wallota sumaro enti wintro   sehstic ur lante,
dar man mih eo scerita   in folc sceotantero:
so man mir at burc ęnigeru   banun ni gifasta,
nu scal mih suasat chind   suertu hauwan,
breton mit sinu billiu,   eddo ih imo ti banin werdan.
doh maht du nu aodlihho,   ibu dir din ellen taoc,
in sus heremo man   hrusti giwinnan,
rauba birahanen,   ibu du dar enic reht habes.'
'der si doh nu argosto   ostarliuto,
der dir nu wiges warne,   nu dih es so wel lustit,
gudea gimeinun: niuse de motti,
hwerdar sih hiutu   dero hregilo rumen muotti,
erdo desero brunnono   bedero uualtan.'
do lettun se aerist   asckim scritan,

'I call on God   above in Heaven
that never did you with such a close kinsman
take things thus'…
He wound from his arm   a winding bracelet,
made of emperor's coin,   which the King gave to him,
the Lord of the Huns: 'This I give to you as a favour.'
Hadubrand spoke,   Hildebrand's son:
'With a spear should a man   receive gifts,
point against point.   …
You are, old Hun,   massively sly,
lure me with your words,   will throw your spear at me.
You are such an old man,   and still you practise cunning.
This was told to me   by sea-farers
coming west across the Wendel Sea,   that battle took him:
dead is Hildebrand,   Heribrand's son.'
Hildebrand spoke,   Heribrand's son:
'Well I can see by your armour
that you have at home   a good lord,
that in this kingdom   you were never an outlaw.' –
'Alas, most powerful God,   an evil fate is coming on us.
I wandered summers and winters,   sixty, out of the land,
when they always placed me   at the fighters' front:
yet never at any place   did the bane seize me.
Now my own child shall   hew me with his sword,
break me with his blade,   or I shall be his bane.
Yet you may easily,   if your courage avails,
from such an old man   win the armour
and gain the prize,   if you have any right.'
'He would be the greatest coward   of the Eastern people,
who would deny you fight,   if you lust after it,
a single combat: let anyone try who can,
whoever today   may boast of this armour,
or of both these breastplates   be the master.'
At this they let   their spears do their task,

21

scarpen scurim: dat in dem sciltim stont.
do stoptun to samane   staimbort chludun,
heuwun harmlicco   huittẹ scilti,
unti im iro lintun   luttilo wurtun,
giwigan miti wabnum […].

in sharp showers   that stuck in the shields.
Then they let their weapons clash   and shattered the war-shields,
hewing embittered   on the gleaming shields,
until the wood   was cut away,
hewn by the weapons […].

… sin tac piqueme,   daz er touuan scal.
uuanta sar so sih diu sela   in den sind arheuit
enti si den lihhamun   likkan lazzit,
so quimit ein heri   fona himilzungalon,
daz andar fona pehhe: dar pagant siu umpi.
sorgen mac diu sela,   unzi diu suona arget,
za uuederemo herie   si gihalot uuerde.
uuanta ipu sia daz Satanazses   kisindi kiuuinnit,
daz leitit sia sar   dar iru leid uuirdit,
in fuir enti in finstri: daz ist rehto uirinlih ding.
upi sia auar kihalont die   die dar fona himile quemant,
enti si dero engilo   eigan uuirdit,
die pringent sia sar uf in himilo rihi:
dar ist lip ano tod,   lioht ano finstri,
selida ano sorgun: dar nist neoman siuh.
denne der man in pardisu   pu kiuuinnit,
hus in himile,   dar quimit imo hilfa kinuok.
pidiu ist durft mihhil
allero manno uuelihemo,   daz in es sin muot kispane,
daz er kotes uuillun   kerno tuo
enti hella fuir   harto uuise,
pehhes pina: dar piutit der Satanasz altist
heizzan lauc.   so mac huckan za diu,
sorgen drato,   der sih suntigen uueiz.
uue demo in uinstri scal   sino uirina stuen,
prinnan in pehhe: daz ist rehto paluuic dink,
daz der man haret ze gote   enti imo hilfa ni quimit.
uuanit sih kinada   diu uuenaga sela:
ni ist in kihuctin   himiliskin gote,
uuanta hiar in uuerolti   after ni uuerkota.
    So denne der mahtigo khuninc   daz mahal kipannit,

24

… the day will dawn   when he will die,
when his soul   will be sent on its way
and when his body   is abandoned;
when comes a host   from Heaven above,
and one from Hell below: and they will battle.
The soul may well worry,   until it has been weighed,
as to which army   it is allotted to.
If it is Satan's   side that wins,
then it is taken   into torment,
to fire and darkness,   a dreadful doom.
If those who come from Heaven   claim it for their own,
then it is assumed   by the angels
who will bring it high   to Heaven's realm:
there is life without death,   light without darkness,
a house without sorrow   where no-one is sick,
for the man in Paradise   has a mansion,
a home in Heaven   that brings help enough.
And so there is a great need
for every man   to make his heart fast,
to do gladly   God's will
and to flee Hell   as hard as he can,
the pain of its fire: here Satan has prepared
hot flame.   May all men heed this
with solemn thought,   all who know they have sinned.
Woe to those who in shadow   do penance for their sins,
burning in flame: that is a fearsome thing
when a man turns to God   and gets no help.
The unworthy soul   believes itself safe
but God in Heaven   does not keep it in grace
because here in the world   it did not do good works.
    So when court is summoned   by the mighty King,

dara scal queman   chunno kilihaz:
denne ni kitar parno nohhein   den pan furisizzan,
ni allero manno uuelih   ze demo mahale sculi.
dar scal er vora demo rihhe   az rahhu stantan,
pi daz er in uuerolti   kiuuerkot hapeta.
   Daz hortih rahhon   dia uueroltrehtuuison,
daz sculi der antichristo   mit Eliase pagan.
der uuarch ist kiuuafanit,   denne uuirdit untar in uuic
   arhapan.
khenfun sint so kreftic,   diu kosa ist so mihhil.
Elias stritit   pi den euuigon lip,
uuili den rehtkernon   daz rihhi kistarkan:
pidiu scal imo helfan   der himiles kiuualtit.
der antichristo   stet pi demo altfiante,
stet pi demo Satanase,   der inan uarsenkan scal:
pidiu scal er in deru uuicsteti   uunt piuallan
enti in demo sinde   sigalos uuerdan.
doh uuanit des uilo… gotmanno
daz Elias in demo uuige   aruuartit uuerde.
so daz Eliases pluot in erda kitriufit,
so inprinnant die perga,   poum ni kistentit
enihc in erdu,   aha artruknent,
muor varsuuilhit sih,   suilizot lougiu der himil.
mano uallit,   prinnit mittilagart,
sten ni kistentit,   uerit denne stuatago in lant,
uerit mit diu uuiru   uiriho uuison:
dar ni mac denne   mak andremo helfan vora demo
   muspille.
denne daz preita uuasal   allaz uarprennit,
enti uuir enti luft   iz allaz arfurpit,
uuar ist denne diu marha,   dar man dar eo mit sinen
   magon piehc?
diu marha ist farprunnan,   diu sela stet pidungan,
ni uueiz mit uuiu puaze: so uerit si za uuize.

26

then every clan   shall come to it:
for no person   would presume to delay,
not any single being   who should be there for trial.
There all shall be judged   by the one judge
for all the works   done in the world.
    I heard it said   by the scholars of world-law
that the Antichrist   shall attack Elijah.
The foe has weapons   and the fight begins
with mighty warriors   for a mighty cause.
Elijah's fight   is for eternal life
and he will rescue the kingdom   for the righteous:
and so he will be helped   by Heaven's powers.
The Antichrist   stands by our ancient foe,
stands by Satan,   who will not save him;
and so he shall fall wounded   on this field of battle
and in this way   will lose the fight.
Yet many...   men of God believe
that Elijah will be wounded   in this event,
so that the blood of Elijah will drip to the earth:
then mountains will burn,   and no tree will be standing
on the earth,   and waters will ebb;
the fens will vanish   and the skies will flame;
the moon will fall and middle earth burn;
no stone will stand   when judgement shows itself,
coming with fire   to find every man:
and no kinship may save   any man from the Muspilli,
for the broad earth   will all burn,
and fire and air   will frazzle:
where is then the march   where a man fought with his kin?
The march is consumed,   the soul stands captured,
and if it does not repent,   then it goes down to Hell.

Pidiu ist demo manne so guot,   denner ze demo
    mahale quimit,
daz er rahono uueliha   rehto arteile.
denne ni darf er sorgen,   denne er ze deru suonu quimit.
ni uueiz der uuenago man,   uuielihan uuartil er habet,
denner mit den miaton   marrit daz rehta,
daz der tiuual dar pi   kitarnit stentit.
der hapet in ruouu   rahono uueliha,
daz der man er enti sid   upiles kifrumita,
daz er iz allaz kisaget,   denne er ze deru suonu quimit.
ni scolta sid manno nohhein   miatun intfahan.
    So daz himilisca horn   kilutit uuirdit,
enti sih der suanari   ana den sind arheuit
der dar suannan scal   toten enti lepenten,
denne heuit sih mit imo   herio meista,
daz ist allaz so pald,   daz imo nioman kipagan ni mak.
denne uerit er ze deru mahalsteti   deru dar kimarchot ist:
dar uuirdit diu suona   dia man dar io sageta.
denne uarant engila   uper dio marha,
uuechant deota,   uuissant ze dinge.
denne scal manno gilih   fona deru moltu arsten.
lossan sih ar dero leuuo uazzon: scal imo auar sin lip
    piqueman,
daz er sin reht allaz   kirahhon muozzi,
enti imo after sinen tatin   arteilit uuerde.
denne der gisizzit,   der dar suonnan scal
enti arteillan scal   toten enti quekkhen:
denne stet dar umpi   engilo menigi,
guotero gomono: gart ist so mihhil:
dara quimit ze deru rihtungu so uilo   dia dar ar resti
    arstent,
so dar manno nohhein   uuiht pimidan ni mak,
dar scal denne hant sprehhan,   houpit sagen,

And so this is only just   that men should come to
    judgement,
and get their deserts   for every grave sin.
There is no point in being careworn,   for that judgement
    will come.
Nor does the sinner know   who will sentence him,
when he breaks the law   with his bribery:
for it is the Devil   who stands and deceives.
He has calculated   every crime
a sinner ever did   before or since,
and he will make it clear   when that day comes;
which is why no man   should make bribery his friend.
    When the heavenly horn   echoes from Heaven
and the Great Judge   goes out on his way
who will deal with   dead and living,
then arises with him   the greatest army,
which is so bold   that no-one can beat it.
Then he goes to the judgement place   which has been
    preordained:
there will be the court,   as countless voices told.
Then the angels will go   across the land,
waking the people   and pointing to the thing-place.
Then shall all men   arise from the dust,
leaving behind the grave's burden   to gain a body,
so that what is right   may be reckoned
and judgement be done   according to deeds.
Then there sits one   who shall judge
and hold a court   of the quick and the dead.
Then many angels   will stand around,
and good men: their number is great.
Then arrive at the judgement so many   who arise from the
    dead.
And no man   may keep any secret:
the hand shall speak   and the head shall say,

allero lido uuelih   unzi in den luzigun uinger,
uuaz er untar desen mannun   mordes kifrumita.
dar ni ist eo so listic man   der dar iouuiht arliugan megi,
daz er kitarnan megi   tato dehheina,
niz al fora demo khuninge   kichundit uuerde,
uzzan er iz mit alamusanu furimegi
enti mit fastun   dio uirina kipuazti.
denne der paldet   der gipuazzit hapet,
denner ze deru suonu quimit.
uuirdit denne furi kilragan   daz frono chruci,
dar der heligo Christ   ana arhangan uuard.
denne augit er dio masun,   dio er in deru menniski anfenc,
dio er durah desse mancunnes   minna fardoleta.

every limb down   to the little finger,
what he did with men,   what murders were committed.
There is no man so cunning   that he could conceal anything,
that he could keep   any deed quiet
which is to be heard   by Heaven's King.
Unless he has given alms
and has fought his sinning   with fasting:
only then may he rest,   if he has repented
when he comes to the Judgement.
Then will be carried   the Cross of the Lord,
on which the holy Christ   was hanged.
Then he will see the marks   Christ received as man,
which he let happen   out of love for men.

DAS LUDWIGSLIED

Rithmus teutonicus de piae memoriae Hluduico rege filio Hluduici aeque regis.

Einan kuning uueiz ih, Heizsit her Hluduig,
  Ther gerno gode thionot: Ih uueiz her imos lonot.
Kind uuarth her faterlos. Thes uuarth imo sar buoz:
  Holoda inan truhtin, Magaczogo uuarth her sin.
Gab her imo dugidi, Fronisc githigini,
  Stuol hier in Vrankon. So bruche her es lango!
Thaz gideilder thanne Sar mit Karlemanne,
  Bruoder sinemo, Thia czala uuunniono.
So thaz uuarth al gendiot, Koron uuolda sin god,
  Ob her arbeidi So iung tholon mahti.
Lietz her heidine man Obar seo lidan,
  Thiot Vrancono Manon sundiono.
Sume sar verlorane Uuurdun sum erkorane:
  Haranskara tholota Ther er misselebeta.
Ther ther thanne thiob uuas, Ind er thanana ginas,
  Nam sina vaston: Sidh uuarth her guot man.
Sum uuas luginari, Sum skachari,
  Sum fol loses, Ind er gibuozta sih thes.
Kuning uuas ervirrit, Thaz richi al girrit,
  Uuas erbolgan Krist: Leidhor, thes ingald iz.
Thoh erbarmedes got, Uuisser alia thia not:
  Hiez her Hluduigan Tharot sar ritan.
'Hluduig, kuning min, Hilph minan liutin!
  Heigun sa Northman Harto biduuungan.'
Thanne sprah Hluduig: 'Herro, so duon ih,
  Dot ni rette mir iz, Al thaz thu gibiudist.'
Tho nam her godes urlub, Huob her gundfanon uf,
  Reit her thara in Vrankon Ingagan Northmannon.
Gode thancodun The sin beidodun,
  Quadhun al: 'fro min, So lango beidon uuir thin.'

32

THE SONG OF LUDWIG

A German poem in pious memory of King Ludwig, whose father Ludwig was also King.

Ludwig King of the Franks defeats the Vikings

I know a King,   who is called Ludwig,
  who gladly serves God: God will give him his reward.
The child lost his father,   but gained another:
  the Lord took him,   the Lord tutored him.
God gave him virtue   and a people that was true,
  and the throne of France: long may he reign!
He divided the land   with Karlmann,
  his kinsman,   as his first action.
When this came to pass,   God put him to the test:
  could the young ruler   cope with trouble?
God let heathen men sail   across the main
  to remind the Franks   that they were a sinful folk.
Some who had been lost   joined the elect.
  Punishment was suffered   by the wicked.
The vagabond   who turned penitent
  and fasted, was numbered   with the good.
Some were oath-breakers,   some were law-breakers,
  some full of vice: and all did penance.
The King was far away,   the Reich in disarray,
  the Christ was angered: the people paid for it.
Yet God had mercy,   for He knew their distress.
  He commanded Ludwig   that he should ride:
'Ludwig, my King: bring help to my kin!
  The men from the north   have harried them hard.'
Then Ludwig gave reply: 'Lord I shall obey,
  and, unless I am killed,   I shall do your will.'
Then he took leave of God   and raised the war-flag.
  He rode into France   to meet the Norsemen.
They thanked God,   those who had bided
  and all said: 'Lord,   for you we have bided long.'

33

Thanne sprah luto   Hluduig ther guoto:
  'Trostet hiu, gisellion,   Mine notstallon.
Hera santa mih god   Ioh mir selbo gibod,
  Ob hiu rat thuhti,   Thaz ih hier gevuhti,
  Mih selbon ni sparoti,   Unc ih hiu gineriti.
Nu uuillih thaz mir volgon   Alle godes holdon.
  Giskerit ist thiu hieruuist   So lango so uuili Krist:
  Uuili her unsa hinavarth,   Thero habet her giuualt.
So uuer so hier in ellian   Giduot godes uuillion,
  Quimit he gisund uz,   Ih gilonon imoz;
  Bilibit her thar inne,   Sinemo kunnie.'
Tho nam er skild indi sper,   Ellianlicho reit her;
  Uuolder uuar errahchon   Sinan uuidarsahchon.
Tho ni uuas iz burolang,   Fand her thia Northman.
  Gode lob sageda,   Her sihit thes her gereda.
Ther kuning reit kuono,   Sang lioth frano,
  Ioh alle saman sungun   'Kyrrieleison'.
Sang uuas gisungan,   Uuig uuas bigunnan,
  Bluot skein in uuangon: Spilodun ther Vrankon.
Thar vaht thegeno gelih,   Nichein soso Hluduig:
  Snel indi kuoni,   Thaz uuas imo gekunni.
Suman thuruhskluog her,   Suman thuruhstah her.
  Her skancta ce hanton   Sinan fianton
  Bitteres lides.   So uue hin hio thes libes!
Gilobot si thiu godes kraft: Hluduig uuarth sigihaft;
  Ioh allen heiligon thanc!   Sin uuarth ther sigikamf.
Uuolar abur Hluduig,   Kuning unser salig!
  So garo soser hio uuas,   So uuar soses thurft uuas,
  Gihalde inan truhtin   Bi sinan ergrehtin.

Then the loud voice   of good Ludwig announced:
    'Be of good heart,   my companions in fate.
God sent me here, and he   himself commanded me
    that, if you deem it right,   here I should stand and fight
    and should not spare myself,   until we are all saved.
Now, this is my desire: that God's saints should follow me,
    for our earthly life   lies in the will of Christ
    and if he desires our death,   then such is his strength.
Whoever with good heart   fulfils the will of God
    and comes out of it alive   will have his reward,
    and, for those who die,   I shall look to their family.'
Then he took shield and spear   and rode as a hero
    desiring to show   the truth to his foes.
Before very long   he found the Norsemen,
    and praised his God   for finding what he sought.
The King rode boldly   and sang piously
    and they all sang: 'Kyrie eleison'.
The song was sung   and battle began
    and cheeks flushed with blood: and how the Franks fought!
All battled with courage,   though none like King Ludwig:
    with power and might,   as befitted his rank.
This man he cut down,   this man he cut through,
    he sent most swiftly   to his enemies
    bitter sufferings: alas for their bodies!
Praise to God's power,   for Ludwig had victory.
    Praise to all the saints!   Ludwig was victorious.
All blessings for Ludwig,   our blessed King!
    As ready as he was,   in the face of distress,
    may the Lord keep him always,   always in his grace.

DE POETA

Dat gafregin ih mit firahim   firiuuizzo meista,
Dat ero ni uuas   noh ufhimil,
noh paum noh pereg ni uuas,
ni sterro nohheinig   noh sunna ni scein,
noh mano ni liuhta,   noh der marco seo.
Do dar niuuiht ni uuas   enteo ni uuenteo,
enti do uuas der eino   almahtico cot,
manno miltisto,   enti dar uuarun auh manake mit inan
cootlihhe geista,   enti cot heilac.

Cot almahtico, du himil enti erda gauuorahtos, enti
du mannun so manac coot forgapi, forgip mir in dino
ganada rehta galaupa enti cotan uuilleon, uuistom enti
spahida enti craft, tiuflun za uuidarstantanne enti arc za
piuuisanne enti dinan uuilleon za gauurchanne.

THE WESSOBRUNN PRAYER

A depiction of the nothingness before creation, followed by a prayer

ON THE CREATOR

That I learned among people   the greatest wonder of all,
that there was no earth   nor Heaven above,
no tree no mountain there was,
no single star   no sun to shine,
no moon that gleamed   nor the glowing sea.
When there was nothing   not end nor wend,
and there was the one   almighty God,
mildest of men,   and there were also many with him
godly ghosts   and holy God.

God almighty, you made Heaven and earth, and you gave
man so many goods: give me in your grace right belief
and good will, wisdom and judgement and strength to
resist the Devil and to avoid evil and to work your will.

Merseburger Zaubersprüche

I

Eiris sazun Idisi   sazun hera duoder.
suma hapt heptidun,   suma heri lezidun,
suma clubodun   umbi cuoniouuidi:
insprinc haptbandun,   inuar uigandun. H.

II

Phol ende Uuodan   uuorun zi holza.
du uuart demo Balderes uolon   sin uuoz birenkit.
thu biguol en Sinthgunt,   Sunna era suister;
thu biguol en Friia,   Uolla era suister;
thu biguol en Uuodan,   so he uuola conda:
sose benrenki,   sose bluotrenki, sose lidirenki:
ben zi bena,   bluot zi bluoda,
lid zi geliden,   sose gelimida sin.

Strassburger Tumbo-Spruch

Tumbo saz in berke   mit tumbemo kinde en arme.
tumb hiez der berch   tumb hiez taz kint:
ter heilego Tumbo   uersegene tivsa uunda.
    Ad stringendum sanguinem.

SPELLS AND BLESSINGS

Eight invocations for eight emergencies

MERSEBURG SPELLS

I

Once sat the Idisi,   sat here and there.
Some bound bonds,   some banished the hoard,
some unpicked   the fetters:
escape fetters,   evade enemies. H.

II

Phol and Wodan   rode into the wood.
and the foal of Balder   sprained its foot.
There Sinthgunt charmed it   and Sunna, her sister;
there Freia charmed it   and Volla, her sister;
there Wodan charmed it   as he well could:
as bone-sprain,   so blood-sprain, so limb-sprain:
bone to bone,   blood to blood,
limb to limb,   that they may be limed.

STRASBOURG STUPID SAYING

Stupid sat on the mountain   with a stupid child in arms.
Stupid was called the mountain.   Stupid was called the child.
Saint Stupid   please bless this wound.
    For the stopping of bleeding.

39

Lorscher Bienensegen

Kirst, imbi ist hucze!   nu fluic du, uihu minaz, hera
fridu frono in godes munt   heim zi comonne gisunt.
Sizi, sizi, bina: inbôt dir sancte maria.
hurolob ni habe du: zi holce ni fluc du,
noh dû mir nindrinnes   noh du mir nintuuinnest.
sizi uilu stillo,   uuirki godes uuillon.

Wurmsegen

Pro nessia.
Gang uz, nesso,   mit niun nessinchilinon,
uz fonna marge in deo adra,   vonna den adrun in daz fleisk,
fonna demu fleiske in daz fel,   fonna demo velle in diz tulli.
   Ter pater noster.

Wiener Hundsegen

Christ uuart gaboren. êr uuolf ode deiob. do uuas sancte
marti christas hirti. der heiligo christ unta sancte marti,
der gauuerdo uualten hiuta dero hunto. dero zohono. daz
in uuolf. noh uualpa za scedin uuerdan nemegi. se uuara
se geloufan uualdes. ode uueges. ode heido. der heiligo
christ unta sancte marti de frumma mir sa hiuto alla hera
heim gasunta.

Lorsch Bee Blessing

Christ, the bees are gone!   Now fly, my pet, along
and peacefully in God's mouth   may you come home safe.
Sit, sit, bee: so commands Saint Mary.
You never had leave   to fly to the wood,
nor to go away   nor to escape from me.
Sit still   and do God's will.

Worm Blessing

Against worms.
Go out worm   with nine wormlings,
out from the bone to the vein,   from the vein to the flesh,
from the flesh to the fur,   from the fur to this tip.
   Three Our Fathers.

Vienna Dog Blessing

Christ was born. Before wolf or thief. Then Saint Martin
was Christ's shepherd. The holy Christ and Saint Martin,
the worthy, may they today take care of our dogs. Of our
bitches. So that neither wolf. Nor she-wolf may bring
harm to them. Wherever they run in the wood. Or on the
way. Or on the heath. The holy Christ and Saint Martin
may they bring me today all of them home and healthy.

Trierer Pferdesegen

Incantacio contra equorum egritudinem quam nos dicimus spurihalz.

Quam Krist endi sancte Stephan zi ther burg Saloniun;
thar uuarth sancte Stephanes hros entphangan. Soso Krist
gibuozta themo sancte Stephanes hrosse thaz entphangana,
so gibuozi ihc it mid Kristes fullesti thessemo hrosse.
Pater noster.
Uuala Krist thu geuuertho gibuozian thuruch thina gnatha
thesemo hrosse thaz antphangana atha thaz spurialza, sose
thu themo sancte Stephanes hrosse gibuoztos zi thero burg
    Saloniun.
Amen.

Züricher Hausbesegnung

Ad signandum domum contra diabolum.

Uuola, uuiht, taz tu uueist,   taz tu uuiht heizist,
Taz tu neuueist noch nechanst   cheden chnospinci.

Trier Horse Blessing

An incantation against the sickness of horses we know as 'spurihalz'.

Came Christ and Saint Stephen to the city Jerusalem;
there was Saint Stephen's horse sprained. As Christ
healed Saint Stephen's horse that was sprained,
so I heal with Christ's help this horse.
Our Father.
So Christ, come down to lead through your grace
this horse that was sprained or that has affliction, just as
you healed Saint Stephen's horse in the city Jerusalem.
Amen.

Zurich House Blessing

For the marking of a house against the Devil.

Important, imp, that it's implied   you are an imp,
that you don't know and cannot   say chnospinci.

VIER VERSE

Hirsch und Hinde

Hirez runeta hintun in daz ora
'uuildi noh, hinta?'

St. Galler Spottvers

Liubene ersatzta sine gruz   unde kab sina tohter uz:
to cham aber Starzfidere,   prahta imo sina tohter uuidere.

Spinnwurtelspruch

veru – taz ist spiz
taz santa tir tin friedel ce minnon.

Hicila-Vers

Hicila diu scona min filu las.

FOUR VERSES

Marginal annotations from the Old High German world

STAG AND HIND

A stag whispered in a hind's ear:
'How about it, hind?'

ST. GALL SATIRE

Liubene brewed his wheat beer   and gave away his daughter.
But then Starzfidere came   and brought her back again.

SPINDLE WHORL SAYING

Veru – that's a point,
sent to you by your bloke, out of love.

HICILA VERSE

Hicila the fair read me often.

MIDDLE HIGH GERMAN VERSE

ANONYM (1)

Dû bist mîn, ich bin dîn.
des solt dû gewis sin.
dû bist beslozzen
in mînem herzen,
verlorn ist das sluzzelîn:
du muost immêr darinne sîn.

ANONYM (2)

Mich dunket nicht sô guotes   noch sô lobesam
sô diu liehte rôse   und diu minne mîns man.
diu kleinen vogellîn
diu singent in dem walde,   dêst menegem herzen liep.
mir enkome mîn holder geselle,   ine hân der
    sumerwunne niet.

ANONYMOUS (1)

Love as imprisonment

You're mine, I'm yours.
Of this you can be sure.
You're imprisoned
in my heart
and, look, we've lost the key.
Nobody's going to set you free.

ANONYMOUS (2)

A lady longs for her lover

I think nothing so good   nor so grand
as the bright rose   and the love of my man.
The very small birds
that sing in the wood are   to other hearts balm.
If my lover doesn't come,   then summer's wonder is
    in vain.

ANONYM (3)

'Mir hât ein ritter,' sprach ein wîp,
'gedienet nâch dem willen mîn.
ê sich verwandelt diu zît,
sô muoz ime doch gelônet sîn.
mich dunket winter unde snê
schoene bluomen unde klê,
swenn ich in umbevangen hân.
und waerz al der werlte leit,
sô muoz sîn wille an mir ergân.'

ANONYMOUS (3)

Love is not to be resisted, even if it defies convention

A woman spoke: 'I have been served
by a knight who fulfilled each wish
and now he shall have his reward,
before any more time shall pass.
To me, the snows and the winter
are like clover and flowers
as long as I have him in my arms.
And, even if the world disapproves,
his wish for me must be my aim.'

Ich zôch mir einen valken   mêre danne ein jâr.
dô ich in gezamete   als ich in wolte hân
und ich im sîn gevidere   mit golde wol bewant,
er huop sich ûf vil hôhe   und fluog in anderiu lant.

Sît sach ich den valken   schône fliegen:
er fuorte an sînem vuoze   sîdîne riemen,
und was im sîn gevidere   alrôt guldîn.
got sende sî zesamene,   die geliep wellen gerne sîn!

Der tunkel sterne   der birget sich,
als tuo dû, vrouwe schoene,   sô du sehest mich,
sô lâ du dîniu ougen gên   an einen andern man.
son weiz doch lützel ieman,   wiez under uns zwein ist getân.

Jô stuont ich nehtint spâte   vor dînem bette,
dô getorste ich dich, frouwe,   niwet wecken.
'des gehazze iemer   got den dînen lîp!
jô enwas ich niht ein eber wilde,'   sô sprach daz waetlîch wîp.

DER VON KÜRENBERG

A story about a falcon

For more than a year   I trained a falcon,
but when I had finished,   when he was tame,
when I had painted   each feather in gold,
he soared high and away   to another land.

Later I saw the falcon   flying free
with silken ribbons   attached to his feet
and every feather painted   gold and red.
May those who want to love   be united by God!

Appearances must be maintained, even when you are in love

The darkened star   now fades away
as you should, lovely lady,   when you see me;
allow your eyes to linger   on other men.
Then no-one will know   what happened.

A bawdy take on courtly love

I stood late at night   before your bed
and, lady, did not dare   to wake you up.
'May God hate you   for evermore!'
the worthy woman said.   'I was no wild boar!'

53

'Slâfest du, friedel ziere?
man wecket uns leider schiere.
ein vogellîn sô wol getân,
daz ist der linden an daz zwî gegân.'

'Ich was vil sanfte entslâfen,
nu rüefestu, kint wâten.
liep âne leit mac niht sîn.
swaz du gebiutest, daz leiste ich, mîn friundîn.'

Diu frouwe begunde weinen:
'du rîtest hinnen und lâst mich eine.
wenne wilt du wider her zuo mir?
ôwê, du füerest mîne fröide sant dir!'

Ez stuont ein frouwe alleine
und warte über heide
und warte ir liebes,
sô gesach si valken fliegen.
'sô wol dir, valke, daz du bist!
du fliugest swar dir liep ist:
du erkiusest dir in dem walde
einen boum, der dir gevalle.
alsô hân ouch ich getân:

DIETMAR VON AIST

Lovers must part at dawn

'Do you sleep, my dearest love?
For soon they will wake us.
The smallest of fair birds
has landed outside on the lime-tree's branch.'

'I was sleeping so softly
and now, my child, you wake me.
Love must know sorrow.
What you demand, dear friend, I shall do.'

The lady began to cry.
'You ride off and leave me here.
When will you ever return?
Oh no, when you go, all joy is gone.'

Envy for a falcon, free in flight

A lady stood by herself,
looking out over the heath
and waiting for her lover.
She saw a flying falcon.
'Falcon, how lucky you are!
You can fly where you want
and can find, in the forest,
the tree on which you can rest.
And I have done the same.

ich erkôs mir selbe einen man,
den erwelten mîniu ougen.
daz nîdent schoene frouwen.
owê, wan lânt si mir mîn liep?
joch engerte ich ir dekeiner trûtes niet!'

I have chosen a man
whom my eyes elected.
By lovely women I am envied.
Oh no, why do they want to take him?
I never tried to take lovers from them!'

Ich var mit iuweren hulden, herren unde mâge,
luit unde lant die müezen saelic sîn.
ez ist unnôt, daz ieman mîner verte vrâge,
ich sage wol für wâr die reise mîn.
mich vienc diu minne und lie mich varn ûf mîne sicherheit.
nu hât sie mir enboten bî ir liebe, daz ich var.
ez ist unwendic, ich muoz endelîchen dar.
wie kûme ich braeche mîne triuwe und mînen eit!

Sich rüemet maniger, waz er dur die minne taete.
wâ sint diu werc? die rede hoere ich wol.
doch saehe ich gern, daz si ir eteslîchen baete,
daz er ir diente, als ich ir dienen sol.
ez ist geminnet, der sich dur die minne ellenden muoz.
nu seht, wie si mich ûz mîner zungen ziuhet über mer.
und lebte mîn her Salatîn und al sîn her
dien braehte mich von Vranken niemer einen fuoz.

Ir minnesinger, iu muoz ofte misselingen,
daz iu den schaden tuot, daz ist der wân.
ich will mich rüemen, ich mac wol von minnen singen,
sît mich diu minne hât und ich sie hân.
daz ich dâ wîl, seht, daz will alse gerne haben mich.
sô müest aber ir verliesen underwîlent wânes vil.
ir ringent umbe liep, daz iuwer niht enwil.
wan müget ir armen minnen solhe minne als ich?

A knight sets out on a crusade to prove his love

I go with your blessing, my lords and my kin.
And so I bless this people and this land.
There's little point in asking me my plan.
Just listen while I tell you where I'm bound.
I'd fallen in love's trap, enslaved to love.
Now I'm asked to go, for love of her.
There's nothing for it: soon I shall be there.
How could I break my honour and my vow?

Many boast of what they would do for love.
Where are their works? I only see words.
I'd really like to see what *they* would give.
I'd like to see if they'd serve as I serve.
The meaning of love is to go far away,
overseas, if such be her command.
And yet I should not stir from my own land
for Saladin and all his mighty army.

You singers of love, your work just deceives.
You have no clue about the things you sing.
I'll praise myself, for I can sing of love,
for love has me and I have it.
What I want to love wants to love me too!
And yet, all your words are empty.
You're fighting for a love that cannot be.
You fools: why not love the way I do?

'Owê, –
Sol aber mir iemer mê
geliuhten dur die naht
noch wîzer danne ein snê
ir lîp vil wol geslaht?
der trouc die ougen mîn.
ich wânde, ez solde sîn
des liehten mânen schîn.
dô tagte ez.

'Owê, –
Sol aber er iemer mê
den morgen hie betagen?
als uns diu naht engê,
daz wir niht durfen klagen:
"owê, nu ist ez tac,"
als er mit klage pflac,
dô er jungest bî mir lac.
dô tagte ez.'

'Owê, –
Sî kuste âne zal
in dem slâfe mich.
dô vielen hin ze tal
ir trehene nider sich.
iedoch getrôste ich sie,
daz sî ir weinen lie
und mich al umbevie.
dô tagte ez.'

HEINRICH VON MORUNGEN

Two lovers recall how they parted at dawn

'Oh no.
Her body lit up my night.
Shall I ever see it again,
lovelier than I'd have believed,
whiter than the snow that had fallen?
It seemed that moonbeams
danced inside the room.
It seemed like a dream.
Day dawned on us.'

'Oh no.
I cannot stand even the thought
that he will never again stay
to see morning. Our hearts will break
whenever night turns into day.
"Oh no. Now the dawn
has finally come."
I watched his tears roll down.
Day dawned on us.'

'Oh no.
She kissed me even as she slept,
more times than I can recall.
I touched her face and found it wet
with tears that sweetly, softly fell
until this woman
held me in her arms
and I kept her warm.
Day dawned on us.'

'Owê, –
daz er sô dicke sich
bî mir ersehen hât!
als er endahte mich,
sô wolt er sunder wât
mich armen schouwen blôz.
ez was ein wunder grôz,
daz in des nie verdrôz.
dô tagte ez.'

Vil süeziu senftiu toeterinne,
war umbe welt ir toeten mir den lîp,
und ich iuch sô herzeclîchen minne,
zwâre vrouwe, vür elliu wîp?
waenent ir, ob ir mich toetet,
daz ich iuch iemer mêr beschouwe?
nein, iuwer minne hât mich des ernoetet,
daz iuwer sêle ist mîner sêle vrouwe.
sol mir hie niht guot geschehen
von iuwerm werden lîbe,
sô muoz mîn sêle iu des verjehen,
dazs iuwerre sêle dienet dort als einem reinen wîbe.

'Oh no.
How many times my lover looked
at me, as if he could not believe
what had been revealed
when he removed what covered me
to take in the scene
of the naked skin
that shone for him alone.
Day dawned on us.'

The lover accuses his beloved

My sweet soft assassin: tell me why
you've decided I shouldn't live
when even you couldn't deny
that you were my one true love.
Do you really think that if you kill me
then you can stop me looking at you?
No, your love continues to thrill me
and your soul is mistress of my soul.
So even if you give me no favours here
from your worthy body,
my soul must assure you
that it will later praise yours as that of a pure lady.

Von den elben wirt entsehen vil manic man,
sô bin ich von grôzer liebe entsên
von der besten, die ie dehein man ze vriunt gewan.
wil aber sî dar umbe mich vên
und ze unstaten stên,
mac si danne rechen sich
und tuo, des ich si bite. sô vreut si sô sê're mich,
daz mîn lîp vor wunnen muoz zergên.

Sî gebiutet und ist in dem herzen mîn
vrowe und hêrer, danne ich selbe sî.
hei wan muoste ich ir alsô gewaltic sîn,
daz si mir mit triuwen waere bî
ganzer tage drî
unde eteslîche naht!
sô verlür ich niht den lîp und al die maht.
jâ ist sie leider vor mir alze vrî.

Mich enzündet ir vil liehter ougen schîn,
same daz viur den durren zunder tuot,
und ir vremeden krenket mir daz herze mîn
same daz wazzer die vil heize gluot.
und ir hôher muot
und ir schoene und ir werdecheit
und daz wunder, daz man von ir tugenden seit,
daz wirt mir vil übel – oder lîhte guot?

Swenne ir liehten ougen sô verkêrent sich,
daz si mir aldur mîn herze sên,
swer dâ enzwischen danne gêt und irret mich,
dem muoze al sîn wunne gar zergên!

By the elves is bewitched so many a man,
and I am bewitched by a love so great,
of the best woman who ever became a friend.
If, for this, I incur her spite
and am dishonoured,
then let her avenge herself,
for that is my will, and such will be the relief,
that wonder will make my very body dead.

She commands and in this poor heart of mine
is sovereign, more than I ever could be.
Ah, if only it were possible for me to attain
an equal power, to make her serve me
for days numbering three
and the same count of nights!
Then I would lose neither spirit nor strength.
Yes, this woman is sadly only too free.

I am set on fire by the gleam of her eyes,
just as the spark lights the dry tinder,
and my heart is hurt by her enmity,
the way that water will hurt the fire.
And her high spirit
and her beauty and her worthiness
and the wonders they tell of her virtues:
this is my curse. Or is it my good?

Whenever her bright eyes turn to me
and see deep down into my heart –
then, if any man should get in between,
I could wish that all his peace would depart!

ich muoz vor ir stên
unde warten der vröiden mîn
rehte alsô des tages diu kleinen vogellîn.
wenne sol mir iemer liep geschên?

I must stand and must wait
in front of her for my joy,
just as small birds wait for the day.
When will I have my reward?

Under der linden
an der heide,
dâ unser zweier bette was,
dâ mugent ir vinden
schône beide
gebrochen bluomen unde gras.
vor dem walde in einem tal,
tandaradei!
schône sanc die nachtigal.

Ich kam gegangen
zuo der ouwe,
dô was mîn friedel komen ê.
dâ wart ich enpfangen
hêre frouwe,
daz ich bin saelic iemer mê.
kust er mich? wol tûstentstunt!
tandaradei!
seht, wie rôt mir ist der munt.

Dô het er gemachet
also rîche
von bluomen eine bettestat.
des wird noch gelachet
innéclîche,
kumt iemen an daz selbe pfat.
bî den rôsen er wol mac,
tandaradei!
merken, wâ mirz houbet lac.

WALTHER VON DER VOGELWEIDE

A lady recalls a secret meeting with her lover

Under the lime-tree
out in the field
that was a bed to us both,
there you will see
that something has trampled
the grass and flowers.
Before the wood, in a vale,
tandaradei,
sweetly sang the nightingale.

I went out walking
to the meadow:
and my man was already there.
He gave me a welcome,
by Jesus and Mary,
that makes me happy for ever and ever.
His kisses? There were a thousand!
Tandaradei!
Just look how my mouth is red!

For there he had made
from richest
flowers a bed for us
and many will laugh
in their hearts
when they come on this.
By the roses is how you may –
tandaradei –
see where my head lay.

69

Daz er bî mir laege,
wessez iemen –
nu enwelle got! – sô schamt ich mich.
wes er mit mir pflaege,
niemer niemen
bevinde daz wan er unt ich
und ein kleinez vogellîn!
tandaradei!
daz mag wol getriuwe sî.

In einem zwîvellîchen wân
was ich gesezzen und gedâhte
ich wolte von ir dienste gân,
wan daz ein trôst mich wider brâhte.
trôst mag ez rehte niht geheizen, owê des!
ez ist vil kûme ein kleinez troestelîn,
sô kleine, swenne ichz iu gesage, ir spottet mîn.
doch fröwet sich lützel iemen, er enwizze wes.

Mich hât ein halm gemachet frô:
er giht ich sül genâde vinden.
ich maz daz selbe kleine strô,
als ich hie vore sach von kinden.
nû hoeret unde merket, ob siz denne tuo:
'si tuot, si entuot, si tuot, si entuot, si tuot.'
swie dicke ichz tete, sô was ie daz ende guot.
daz troestet mich: dâ hoeret ouch geloube zuo.

If someone found out,
then, God preserve me, I'd be shamed.
May nobody
ever find out what he did
to me, apart from one very small bird,
and me, and him.
Tandaradei.
I think the bird will keep stumm.

A lover weighs up the advantages and disadvantages of being in love

In a state of hopeful despair
I was sitting and thinking
about leaving my service to her,
but was held by one consolation,
though the word, I fear, is far too strong
for what was at best a small spark:
so small that – if I told you – you'd mock.
But drowning people always clutch at straws.

My straw was found in the field.
It said I would be rewarded.
I plucked this same small plant
to play the game that children played.
So listen and tell me if she really loves me.
'She loves me… not; she loves me… not.'
And every time I played, the end was good.
This comforts me: it all comes down to belief.

Swie liep sie mir von herzen sî,
sô mac ich nu doch wol erlîden
daz ir sîn ie die besten bî.
ich darf ir werben dâ niht nîden.
ich enmac, als ich erkenne, des gelouben niht
daz si ieman sanfte in zwîvel bringen müge.
mir ist liep daz die getrogenen wizzen waz si trüge,
und alze lanc dazs iemer rüemic man gesiht.

Saget mir ieman, waz ist minne –
weiz ich des ein teil, sô west ich es gerne mê.
der sich rehte nu versinne,
der berihte mich, durch wie si tuot sô wê.
minne ist minne, tuot si wol;
tuot si wê, sône enheizet si niht minne.
sus enweiz ich, wie si denne heizen sol.

Ob ich rehte râten künne
waz die minne sî, sô sprechent denne jâ.
minne ist zweier herzen wünne:
teilent sie gelîche, sô ist diu minne dâ.
sol sie aber ungeteilet sîn,
sô enkan sie ein herze aleine niht enthalden.
owê, woltest du mir helfen, frowe mîn!

Frowe, ich trage ein teil ze swaere,
wellest du mir helfen, sô hilf an der zît.
sî aber ich dir gar unmaere,

No matter how much I love her,
I can easily accept
that the best men surround her,
and I do not envy those who press suit.
I find it, in truth, hard to believe
that anyone could be brought to despair
– they must know what they're about – by her,
though it is quite a crowd that sings her praise.

Love's philosophy

What is love? Can anyone tell me?
I know very little and need to know more.
If you're an expert, please help me
to see why love has to wield such power.
Love is love when it does good
and if it hurts, then love it cannot be.
Then I wouldn't know what it was called.

If I'm correct, though, in my guess
about what love is, then let me hear.
Love is the miracle of two hearts
and if they share, then this is love, for sure.
Yet if there's no sharing,
then a single heart will not be enough.
Oh no, please help me, my lady!

Lady, the burden I carry is too great,
so if you want to help me, do it now.
But if you remain indifferent

daz sprich endelîche: so lâze ich den strît
und wirde ein ledic man.
du solt aber einez wizzen: daz dich rehte
lützel ieman baz danne ich geloben kan.

Kan mîn frowe süeze siuren?
waenet sie, daz ich gebe lieb umbe leit?
sol ich si dar umbe tiuren,
daz si sich kêre gar an mîne unwerdekeit?
sô kunde ich unrehte spehen.
wê waz sprich ich ôrenlôser ougen âne?
den diu minne blendet, wie mac der gesehen?

Aller werdekeit ein füegerinne,
daz sît ir zewâre, frouwe Mâze.
ein saelic man, der iuwer lêre hât!
der endarf sich iuwer beschamen inne
beide ze hove noch an der strâze.
dur daz sô suoche ich iemer iuwern rât,
daz ir mich ebene werben lêret.
wirbe ich nidere, wirbe ich hôh, ich bin versêret.
ich was vil nâch ze nidere tôt,
nû bin ich aber ze hôhe siech,
unmâze enlâzet mich ân nôt.

Nideriu minne heizet diu sô swachet,
daz der lîp nâch kranker liebe ringet:
diu minne tuot unlobelîche wê.

then make it clear and I'll renounce war
and become a free man again.
But there's one thing you should know: that, truly,
nobody can praise you better than I can.

Can my lady make bitterness sweet?
Does she think I'll pay back sorrow with joy?
When every single compliment
gets turned by her into misery?
Maybe I don't see this aright.
What am I saying? I have not ears or eyes.
To be blinded by love is to lose your sight.

High love, low love and Lady Moderation

You hold every value in its place,
and this is true, Lady Moderation.
Who follows your counsel will be happy.
He will never need to be ashamed,
whether at court or whether at home,
and this is why I ask you to advise me,
so you can teach me how to pledge my heart.
If I aim too high or low – I'm wounded.
Aiming too low almost killed me!
Now I aim too high and I'm sick again!
False moderation knows no mercy.

Low love is the sort that makes me weak,
when I wrestle for a joy that's diseased:
this love hurts more than you'd believe.

hôhe minne heizet diu daz machet,
daz der muot nâch werder liebe ûf swinget:
diu winket mir nû, daz ich ir mite gê.
nun weiz ich, wes diu mâze beitet.
kumt herzeliebe, sô bin ich verleitet.
doch hât mîn lîp ein wîp ersehen,
swie minneclîche ir rede sî,
mir mac wol schade von ir geschehen.

Ich saz ûf eime steine
und dahte bein mit beine,
dar ûf satzt ich den ellenbogen;
ich hete in mîne hant gesmogen
daz kinne und ein mîn wange.
dô dâhte ich mir vil ange,
wie man zer welte solte leben.
deheinen rât kond ich gegeben,
wie man driu dinc erwurbe,
der keines niht verdurbe.
diu zwei sint êre und varnde guot,
daz dicke ein ander schaden tuot.
daz dritte ist gotes hulde,
der zweier übergulde.
die wolte ich gerne in einen schrîn:
jâ leider desn mac niht gesîn,
daz guot und weltlich êre
und gotes hulde mêre
zesamene in ein herze komen.
stîg unde wege sint in benomen;

High love is the other sort, which makes
my spirit strive for a joy that's exalted:
I should follow her now, seeing her wave.
I know why Moderation's lost for words.
My sweetheart's here: at once I am seduced.
And when, as now, I come across a woman
whose conversation sparkles with its wit,
I know that she can only do me harm.

This world is going to the dogs

I sat down on a rock
and put leg over leg,
on which I put my elbow,
the better then to cradle
my chin and one of my cheeks,
then I started to reflect
how we should live in this world,
but no answer was to be found
as to how we can gain three things,
without one of them going wrong.
Two are honour and worldly goods,
which are each to each often opposed;
the third is divine grace,
which retains third place.
I should like them in a casket
but fear that will never happen:
possessions and the world's honour,
and God's grace, which is more,
coming together in one heart.
Highways and byways are lost.

untriuwe ist in der sâze,
gewalt vert ûf der strâze,
fride unde reht sint sêre wunt.
diu driu enhabent geleites niht,
diu zwei enwerden ê gesunt.

Owê war sint verswunden   alliu mîniu jâr?
ist mir mîn leben getroumet   oder ist ez wâr?
daz ich ie wânde daz   iht waere, was daz iht?
dar nâch hân ich geslâfen   und enweiz es niht.
nû bin ich erwachet,   und ist mir unbekant
daz mir hie vor was kündic   als mîn ander hant.
liut unde lant, dâ ich   von kinde bin erzogen,
die sint mir frömde worden,   reht als ez sî gelogen.
die mîne gespilen wâren,   die sint traege unt alt:
verreitet ist daz velt,   verhouwen ist der walt.
wan daz daz wazzer vliuzet   als ez wîlent flôz,
für wâr ich wânde mîn   ungelücke wurde grôz.
mich grüezet maneger trâge,   der mich bekande ê wol.
diu welt ist allenthalben   ungenâden vol.
als ich gedenke an manigen   wünneclîchen tac
die mir sint enpfallen gar   als in daz mer ein slac,
iemer mêre owê.

Owê wie jaemerlîche   junge liute tuont!
den ê vil hovelîchen   ir gemüete stuont,
die kunnen niuwan sorgen: owê wie tuont si sô?
swar ich zer welte kêre,   dâ ist nieman frô;
tanzen, lachen, singen   zergât mit sorgen gar,

Betrayal is everywhere you look
and violence rules every road:
peace and law carry mortal wounds
and if these two do not recover
then the other three are doomed.

This world has gone to the dogs; could a crusade be the answer?

Alas, where have vanished   all of my years?
Is my life real   or is it a dream?
All that I believed: did it exist?
Perhaps I was asleep   and never knew it.
Now I am awake   and cannot fathom
what I knew so well   like this, my palm.
The people and the land   I knew when I was young
have all become as strange   as if it were undone.
Children I played with   are weary and old.
The woods are cut down   and the fields are burned.
Only the river flows   where it used to flow
and this fact alone   helps me bear my sorrow.
Many men who knew me   can now scarcely greet me
and the whole wide world   seems to lack charity.
When I think back   to many wondrous days,
they have gone like the ripple   of a stone in the lake.
Alas for evermore.

Alas, how miserably   the young people act
who were once so courteous   in all they did.
All they know is sorrow: why is it so?
Nobody is happy   no matter where I go.
Dance, laughter, song   are all cast down.

nie kein kristenman gesach   sô jaemerlîche schar.
nû merket, wie den frouwen   ir gebende stat;
die stolzen ritter tragent   dörpellîche wât.
uns sint unsenfte brieve   her von rôme komen:
uns ist erloubet trûren   und fröide gar benomen.
daz müet mich inneclîchen: wir lebten ê vil wol,
daz ich nû für mîn lachen   weinen kiesen sol.
die vogel in der wilde   betrüebet unser klage:
was wunders ist, ob ich   dâ von an fröiden gar verzage?
wê waz spriche ich tumber   durch mînen boesen zorn?
swer dirre wünne volget   hât jene dort verlorn,
iemer mêr owê.

Owê wie uns mit süezen   dingen ist vergeben!
ich sihe die bittern gallen   in dem honege sweben.
diu welt ist ûzen schoene   wîz, grüen unde rôt
und innân swarzer varwe,   vinster sam der tôt.
swen si nû habe verleitet,   der schouwe sînen trôst:
er wirt mit swacher buoze   grôzer sünde erlôst.
dar an gedenket, ritter,   ez ist iuwer dinc:
ir traget die liehten helme   und manegen herten rinc,
dar zuo die vesten schilte   und diu gewîhten swert!
wolte got wan waere ich   der segenunge wert!
sô wolte ich nôtic armman   verdienen rîchen solt.
joch meine ich niht die huoben   noch der hêrren golt;
ich wolte saelden krône   êweclîchen tragen,
die mohte ein soldenaere   mit sîme sper bejagen,
möht ich die lieben reise   gevaren über sê,
sô wolte ich denne singen wol   und niemer mêr owê,
niemer mêr owê!

Did ever Christian see   such a lamentable crowd?
Look at how fine ladies   are tying up their hair!
Look at how proud knights   are dressed like villagers!
And unkind letters   have come to us from Rome.
Joy is taken from us.   All we may do is mourn.
I know distress within: we used to live so well.
Laughter's in the past   and weeping must prevail.
The birds within the wood   lament our plight
and it will be a wonder   if I don't lose my spirits.
Alas, I am indeed a fool   to utter words in anger.
To gain joy down here   is to lose it in Heaven.
Alas for evermore.

Alas, how we've been poisoned   by the sweetest things.
I see the bitter gall   floating in honey.
The world appears lovely,   all white, and green, and red,
but inwardly it's black,   and darker than death.
Whoever's led astray   may find consolation
and, for great sins,   do an easy penance.
Think of it, you knights,   for this task is yours.
You bear bright armour   with many strong rings,
and a sturdy shield   and a sword that is holy.
I wish to God   that I were only worthy,
that I, a poor man,   might earn a rich reward.
I don't mean land   or the gold of lords,
but I mean a crown,   for all eternity,
which men-at-arms   could win with weaponry.
If I could cross the sea   on the most blessed of travels,
my song would be of joy   and never 'alas'.
Alas for nevermore!

'Sîne klâwen
durch die wolken sint geslagen,
er stîget ûf mit grôzer kraft.
ich sih in grâwen
taegelîch, als er wil tagen,
den tac, der im geselleschaft
erwenden wil, dem werden man,
den ich mit sorgen în bî naht verliez.
ich bringe in hinnen, ob ich kan.
sîn vil manigiu tugent mich daz leisten hiez.'

'Wahtaer, du singest,
daz mir manige fröide nimt
unde mêrt mîne klage.
maer du bringest,
der mich leider niht gezimt,
immer morgens gegen dem tage.
diu solt du mir verswîgen gar.
daz gebiut ich den triuwen dîn.
des lôn ich dir als ich getar,
sô belîbet hie der geselle mîn.'

'Er muoz et hinnen
balde und ân sûmen sich:
nu gip im urloup, suozez wîp.
lâze in minnen
her nâch sô verholn dich,
daz er behalte êre unde den lîp.
er gap sich mîner triuwen alsô
daz ich in braehte ouch wider dan.
ez ist nu tac: naht was ez dô
mit drucken an die bruste dîn kus mir in an gewan.'

WOLFRAM VON ESCHENBACH

Drama at dawn as a watchman attempts to warn two lovers

'Its claws
have sliced the clouds
and it rises with great power.
I see dawn.
Its grey light announces
that day is here. It takes away
the worthy man I smuggled in
by night, obliged by his great state.
I will get him away if I can.
He must leave the company he sought.'

'Watchman, your song
takes away all my joy
and adds to what I suffer.
The news you bring
makes me unhappy
this morning, as I see day appear.
You should not have told me this.
I command you on your honour:
my lover shall not be dismissed.
And you shall have what I can afford.'

'He must leave
soon, and without delay:
sweet lady, say farewell.
Later, he may love
you in secrecy,
to save his honour and his head.
He gave himself to my trust
and I shall get him out of here.
Now it is day. Then it was night.
Your kiss and your embrace gave him to me.'

'Swaz dir gevalle,
wahtaer, sinc, und lâ den hie,
der minne brâht und minne enpfienc.
von dînem schalle
ist er und ich erscrocken ie.
sô ninder der morgenstern ûf gienc
ûf in, der her nâch minne ist komen,
noch ninder lûhte tages lieht,
du hâst in dicke mir benomen
von blanken armen, und ûz herzen niht.'

Von den blicken
die der tac tet durch diu glas,
und dô wahtaere warnen sanc,
si muose erschricken
durch den, der dâ bî ir was.
ir brustlîn an brust si dwanc.
der rîter ellens niht vergaz;
(des wold in wenden wahtaers dôn):
urloup nâh und nâher baz
mit kusse und anders gap in minne lôn.

'Say what you like,
watchman, but leave him here.
He brought me love and love I gave.
When you sing,
he and I are filled with fear.
Before the morning star first shone
on him, who came for love's sake,
before day first showed its light,
you often took him from the embrace
of my white arms – but not from my heart.'

But the rays
that day sent through the window
and the watchman's warning
made her afraid
for her concealed lover.
She pressed her dainty breasts to him.
Despite the way the watchman warned,
the knight recalled that he was man.
Departure neared as daylight dawned
and gave them kisses, and other things.

Der winter ist zergangen,
das prüeve ich ûf der heide.
aldar kan ich gegangen:
guot wart mîn ougenweide

Von den bluomen wolgetân.
wer sach ie sô schoenen plân?
der brach ich zeinem kranze;
den truog ich mit tschoie zuo den frouwen an dem tanze.
well ieman werden hôchgemuot, der hebe sich ûf die schanze!

Dâ stât vîôl unde klê,
sumerlaten, gamandrê,
die werden zîtelôsen;
ôstergloien vant ich dâ, die liljen und die rôsen.
dô wunschte ich, das ich sant mîner frouwen solde kôsen.

Si gab mir an ir den prîs,
das ich waere ir dulz âmîs
mit dienste disen meien:
dur si sô wil ich reien.

TANNHÄUSER

It is spring and time to fall in love

The winter has left us now,
as I can see from the heath,
for I have just been out,
and could not believe my eyes

at the flowers' great beauty.
Who saw such a great display?
I made of them a garland
and took it with joy to the ladies at the dance.
And you should join in too, if you fancy your chance.

There are violets and clover,
willow-shoots, germanders,
and noble crocuses.
Narcissi I found there, lilies and roses.
How I should like to find there my lady's caress!

The prize she awarded me
was to be her *doux ami*
and serve her all this summer.
I shall write dances for her.

Ein kneht, der lag verborgen,
bî einer dirne er slief,
unz ûf den liehten morgen.
der hirte lûte rief:
'wol ûf, lâz ûz die hert!'
des erschrak diu dirne
und ir geselle wert.

Daz strou, daz muost er rûmen
und von der lieben varn.
es torste sich niht sûmen,
er nam si an den arn.
daz höi, daz ob im lag,
daz ersach diu reine
ûf fliegen in den dag.

Davon si muoste erlachen,
ir sigen diu ougen zuo.
sô suoze kunde er machen
in dem morgen fruo
mit ir daz bettespil.
wer sach ân geraete
ie fröiden mê so vil!

Love outside the court

A servant once lay hidden,
sleeping with the maid.
And then appeared the morning.
The cowherd loudly cried:
'Come on, let out the herd!'
His screeches scared the girl,
and her most worthy beau.

The straw was then forsaken.
The lover left his maid.
The servant had to hasten,
no time for love's embrace.
What covered him, the hay,
so the pure girl observed,
flew off into the day.

The maid was seized with laughter,
and softly closed her eyes.
So sweetly he had been her
partner in new day's
game – the one that's played in bed.
Whoever saw such joy,
when life was limited?

The cover illustration is from the Codex Manesse.

Old High German Verse

The titles of the source text poems are in New High German and have been given by scholars.

'The Song of Hildebrand': the manuscript, in two hands, has been dated to around 800. Other poems in the Indo-European tradition, as well as poetic evidence in the text, indicate that Hildebrand will kill his son. Hildebrand and Dietrich appear in the *Nibelungenlied* and other works as heroic figures. Odoacer deposed the last Emperor of Rome, Romulus, in 476. Each man presumably throws only one spear: that they are recorded as flying 'in sharp showers' is due to an Indo-European expression used in heroic poetry.

'Muspilli': the manuscript dates from the ninth century. The poem has been interpreted as a Christianisation of the pagan *Ragnarök*, the end of the world. It has been named for the word *Muspilli* which occurs in it (and nowhere else in Old High German) to signify the Apocalypse, a word left here untranslated, as its meaning is uncertain. Possibly its etymology is 'mouth destruction'. The 'thing-place' was where tribal justice was administered.

'The Song of Ludwig': Louis III of France led the Franks to victory over the Vikings at the Battle of Saucourt-en-Vimeu in 881. Louis died in 882, falling from his horse while in pursuit of a woman, so that the poem can be dated around this time as it is written in the present tense but refers to the King's death in the motto. The *Ludwigslied*, whilst clearly Christian, is in genre an Indo-European song of praise for a great hero.

'*The Wessobrunn Prayer*': from a manuscript around 814, and not just a prayer but a poem as well. The poem can be related to Indo-Germanic traditions and is paralleled in the Sanskrit *Rigveda*, 10.129.

'*Spells and Blessings*': all from tenth-century manuscripts documenting older traditions.

I

'Merseburg Spells': these two spells represent the only direct invocation of pre-Christian deities in Old High German literature. The Idisi of the first spell are goddesses who may aid or oppose humans, possibly Valkyries. The final 'H.' may represent the name of the person whose release is desired.

II

'Strasbourg Stupid Saying': this incantation to stop bleeding shows a linguistic misunderstanding. The Latin word *stupidus* in a source text, indicating paralysis, has been taken to signify 'stupid'. I resisted the temptation to write a prayer to 'Saint Dumbo'.

III

'Lorsch Bee Blessing': part of a long tradition. The swarming of bees raised complicated legal questions of possession.

IV

'Worm Blessing': the worms are requested to go into an arrow held at the foot of a horse (or possibly into the hoof), where they will be harmless.

V

'Vienna Dog Blessing': a shepherd's prayer. The saint invoked is Martin of Tours.

VI

'Trier Horse Blessing': an incantation against the infirmity *spurihalz*, some unspecified lameness.

'Zurich House Blessing': a great deal of scholarship has been devoted to interpreting the final word of the blessing, *chnospinci*. I follow Müller, who sees it as a nonsense word, difficult to pronounce, that will puzzle the evil spirit, and I retain it in the translation, although it would be possible to think up English nonsense words that fulfil the same function.

'Four Verses': Müller categorises the first three as reflections of ordinary life, marginal annotations by bored monks. The first, accompanied by musical notation, was probably a dance, with clear erotic overtones. The second makes fun of Liubene, whose daughter is returned to him, perhaps because she is infertile, which would invalidate a marriage. The third verse can be taken as a lust lyric, playing on an ancient tradition. These three verses date from the eleventh, ninth and ninth/tenth centuries respectively. The final eleventh-century verse may refer to the Empress Gisela, a friend of the theological writings of Notker, monk of the Abbey of St. Gall, where it was written, making it the first book to speak German.

MIDDLE HIGH GERMAN VERSE

The poems are untitled.

ANONYMOUS (1)-(3): three poems by unidentified authors. The first poem has been widely anthologised on account of its simple and direct approach. The second and third poems, like others in the anthology, are written solely from the point of view of the woman, another indication of why the narrator of *Minnesang* should not be identified with the poet, who was engaged in a highly stylised public performance, as discussed in the Introduction.

DER VON KÜRENBERG: active in the middle of the twelfth century.

DIETMAR VON AIST: active in the middle of the twelfth century. The first poem given here is a *Tagelied* [dawn song], in which lovers are parted by the dawning day. There are other examples in the anthology.

HARTMANN VON AUE: active 1180-1205. Author of the important courtly romances *Erec* and *Iwein,* and of the courtly legends *Der arme Heinrich* [Poor Heinrich] and *Gregorius.*

HEINRICH VON MORUNGEN: d. 1220. One of the greatest of the *Minnesänger.*

WALTHER VON DER VOGELWEIDE: c. 1170-1230. Walther's lyrics are some of the most celebrated in the canon. He wrote political songs as well as *Minnesang*: the final poem here functions as a call to participate in the crusade of the Holy Roman Emperor Frederick II, whose excommunication is referred to in the 'unkind letters' from Rome in the second stanza.

WOLFRAM VON ESCHENBACH: active 1200-1220, he produced the Grail legend *Parzivâl*, the apotheosis of the courtly romance, and the epic *Willehalm.*

TANNHÄUSER: died after 1265. The legend of his sojourn with Venus is the subject of the opera *Tannhäuser* by Wagner. The French expression *doux ami* in the fourth stanza means 'gentle friend'.

STEINMAR: active 1270-80. His depiction of a less than courtly scene – a take on the *Tagelied* – is an interesting end to this anthology.

ABOUT THE TRANSLATOR

PHILIP WILSON grew up in Yorkshire and went on to work in comprehensive schools before turning to literary translation in the form of an MA and a PhD at the University of East Anglia, where he now teaches literature, translation and philosophy, after a spell at İnönü University, Malatya, Turkey. He has translated *The Luther Breviary* (with John Gledhill) and has edited *Literary Translation: Re-drawing the Boundaries* (with Jean Boase-Beier and Antoinette Fawcett). The monograph *Translation after Wittgenstein* will be published in 2015. He has published many poems in magazines, as well as a pamphlet, *Blessed and not broken by the fall.*

He lives in Norwich and his interests include graphic novels, early music and the relationship between translation and mysticism. The Old and Middle High German texts in this volume have remained a constant source of fascination since he first encountered them as an undergraduate.

ROGNVALDR KALI KOLSSON, EARL OF ORKNEY
Crimsoning the Eagle's Claw
Selected, translated from the Old Norse
and introduced by Ian Crockatt
with a Preface by Kevin-Crossley Holland

CHARLES BAUDELAIRE
Selected Poems from Les Fleurs du Mal
Translated from the French by Jan Owen
and introduced by Rosemary Lloyd

Further titles of poetry in translation are available in
'Arc Visible Poets', 'Arc Translations', 'Arc Anthologies' and
'New Voices from Europe & Beyond' (anthologies)

www.arcpublications.co.uk